Yesteryear in Masontown
And Surrounding Communities,
Volume I

by Marci Lynn McGuinness

Published by Shore Publications (Formerly Backwoods Books)
P. O. Box 26, Chalk Hill, PA 15421

Copyright © May 1994
Second Printing 2008

ISBN 10: 0-938833-09-X
ISBN 13: 978-0-938833-09-3

More *Yesteryear* and regional books at:
www.ohiopyle.info
shorepublications@yahoo.com

FORWARD

Dear Yesteryear Readers:

Since the publication of the Yesteryear in Ohiopyle Calendar/Book set in the fall of '93, the Yesteryear series has developed with Yesteryear in Masontown being book/calendar set 2.

Upcoming Yesteryear books/calendars for 1994-95 are: Yesteryear in Ohiopyle, Volume II, Yesteryear in Connellsville, Yesteryear in Point Marion and Smithfield Area, and Yesteryear on the National Road.

After receiving much help and co-operation from the German-Masontown library staff, local historians and photo contributors, I would like to thank all who encouraged this project.

Recording history cannot be done alone: a researcher needs proud, knowledgeable people to guide him/her toward correct information.

As I compile and write Yesteryear in Ohiopyle, Volume II for publication in July, I continue to collect old photos, books, and newspapers concerning the local history of Fayette County and neighboring villages with the goal being the preservation of as much Fayette County history as is humanly possible.

The response born out of Yesteryear in Ohiopyle Volume I tells me that this is a viable project to continue.

Special thanks to Buzzy Duritza and Spellman Studio for all their help in restoring the old photographs.

Thanks so much for your support and interest!

Marci Lynn McGuinness
Publisher
Backwoods Books

My Sincere Thanks To The Following Contributors:
Without You This Book Would Not Have Become A Reality.

Gail Cunningham and The Staff
At The German-Masontown Public Library

Fort Mason Historical Society

Russ King and the Masontown Fire Department

Telio Packroni • Tom McArdle • Pete Smargie

Carl Wheeler • J. R. Rhoades • Nancy and Virginia Wilson
Joe Stoffa • Charles Chuiko • Dorothy Rice • Dan Girard
Nancy Zapatosky • Mary Lacona • Saul Lowe • Edith Magalotti
Tim Berkshire • Paul Verska • Dorothy Jesso • Mr. & Mrs. Frank Bartoroni
Roye Leckemby • Helen Gosh • Francis Mullooly • Chuck Grimm
Thomas Kaprive • Joe Ferary • Martha Dorsey • Shawn Culleton
Carmine Guappone • Steve Halowich • Clark Dearth • George Lilley
Orris Bizub • Alwida Murphy • Laura Ferranti • Dan Vidovich
Frances Havens • Martha Lardin Gapen • Mae Thomas
David McElroy • Ben Gapen • Joe Micoli • Ed Dunlevy
Rich Barron • Nancy Oravets • Lou Albani

CONTENTS

YESTERYEAR IN MASONTOWN .... PAGE 1

DOWNTOWN MASONTOWN .... PAGE 2

MASONTOWN FIRE DEPARTMENT .... PAGE 30

THE PAL'S CLUB .... PAGE 41

YESTERYEAR IN NEW GENEVA .... PAGE 59

YESTERYEAR WITH ALBERT GALLATIN AT FRIENDSHIP HILL .... PAGE 63

YESTERYEAR IN BESSEMER .... PAGE 69

YESTERYEAR IN PALMER .... PAGE 84

YESTERYEAR IN McCLELLANDTOWN .... PAGE 86

YESTERYEAR IN FOOTEDALE .... PAGE 88

YESTERYEAR PEOPLE .... PAGE 99

MASONTOWN'S OLD TIMES - Poem by Everella Virginia Neff .... PAGE 105

BIBLIOGRAPHY .... PAGE 121

Yesteryear in Masontown

For centuries before the Delaware and Shawnee Indians lived in the Masontown area, the "Mound Builders" resided, worked and worshipped here along the river. The Mound Builders are the first known local inhabitants having come here well before 500 A.D., when farming and crafts began to invade their simple lives of hunting, fishing, and seed gathering. We call them the Mound Builders because they carried baskets of earth on their heads, dumping them together until enormous mounds were erected. Here they built the chief's houses, buried their dead, or threw animal remains, shells and the like. Many were used as religious temples. Today, two mounds still remain here. One is located at the Route 166 and 266 intersection north of New Geneva; the other on Route 266 2 miles from New Geneva on the Conn farm. The Mound Builders were later known for their pottery achievements.

The area then became the hunting ground for Iroquois and the home of Delaware and Shawnee Indians fleeing the Iroquois. It is said that Chief Cornstalk lived at Gray's Landing when he led the Indians during the battle of Point Pleasant, Virginia in 1774.

During the 1730's, French and English tradesmen began coming to the area. Mr. Wendill Brown and his sons are said to have settled between Gray's Landing and Martin around 1751, where they packed meat and corn, supplying George Washington's troops in 1754 at the Great Meadows.

In 1780, John Mason built "Fort Mason" just east of the town. Early settlers went to the shelter for safety during trouble with the Indians. In 1823, the fort was given to Mr. John Debolt by Ephraim Walter. Debolt had it moved to Main Street. It was at the old fort that the Whiskey Boys of 1794 rallied around their liberty pole during the days of the insurrection. A well known musician, Seth Ely, lived at the new site for many years. This is where today's Masonic Building stands. It was built in 1903.

SHAWNEE CHIEF CORNSTALK

"Monongahela, Pure Rye" Whiskey gained lasting fame during the 1780's. The men — Gilmore, Work, and Rabb — owned many mills, first on local creeks and then along the river. Rabb soon began building keel boats along with other businessmen and shipping whiskey and flour to New Orleans on them. Rabb made a fortune by hiring a man named Dunlevy, a talented distiller who never gave out his secret for getting a yield of two and three-eighths gallons of whiskey per bushel of grain.

John Debolt was the first to use a steam engine to power a mill in the area. He bought the engine for $900 in 1833 from Cuthbertson & Roe of Brownsville. In 1823, Debolt started a low (but satisfactory) quality pottery in Masontown.

Masontown was formerly called "Germantown". It was laid out on a tract of land called East Abington by John Mason on May 29, 1798. The deed conveyed to the residents the usual privileges and franchises stated in town charters within its streets and alleys. In 1801, John and Apalonia Mason gave the town a house and a lot on Water Street designated for the purpose of a school intending to give "An education — German and English — in the Arts and Sciences, Morality, and Religion." This was the first effort for a public school system here. Lawrence Rider and Solomon Overturf were trustees.

William (Big Bill) Laughead was the town's first postmaster. He began his job in 1840 receiving mail by The Pony Express once a week. Because of the hardships involved in transporting the U.S. Mail, it cost $5.00 to mail a letter at that time!

The first store was opened in Masontown by Jesse Ross in 1847. John Sterling soon built the Altman House and then the Leroy Hotel, in honor of his son who had passed on.

During the Civil War, Masontown was part of the Union Territory. Republicans were against slavery and Democrats held other views. Following the war, veterans brought a cannon home and placed it atop what is now known as Cannon Hill. After the election, the Republicans beat the Democrats badly, and held their celebration on Cannon Hill. This angered the Democrats so that a group of them got together during the night and rolled the cannon down to the ferry, loaded it up and dumped it in the river just opposite Whitely Creek, where today's power plant sits.

In 1876, at the March session of court, Masontown was incorporated into a borough. John Hyde was elected borough constable at this time. It is said that he was not well versed on law and order and was often physically removed from the borough when trying to make arrests.

In 1900 Masontown's first bank was opened with Alex Mack as President. In 1913-1914 the roads were bricked.

It was July 20, 1909, when the great fire of Masontown destroyed a block of businesses. It began in a small building next to the Altman Hotel, but without fire hydrants or a fire department, the men were hard pressed to fight the growing flames. After many attempts to stop the fire from spreading, including using dynamite in neighboring buildings, Lloyd Ramsey brought sheet-iron from his tin shop and nailed them to the bank's windows and to the home of Mr. H. A. Johnson.

During the seven hour fire, $225,000 worth of property was destroyed. The burnt buildings included were the Altman Hotel, Charlie Sangston's frame structure, Frank Madas' Meat Market, the First National Bank, Jesse Sterling's Grocery Store, and a building owned by Ray Anderson. There was also damage to buildings across the street by way of broken plate glass windows and scorched outer walls.

In the wake of this disaster, sturdier buildings were constructed including a new bank, the New Mason Hotel, the new Anderson Building, and the Rex Theatre. In 1911 water and sewage plants were also installed.

The oldest continuous religious denomination in Masontown is the Methodist, which began in 1820, followed by the Presbyterian established in 1840, the Brethren in 1882, All Saints Roman Catholic 1908, and St. Mary's Orthodox in 1910. The town's first fire department was established in 1924 on North Water Street.

For decades, residents were dependent on the coal and coke industries, which faded out during the fifties, forcing miners to travel to neighboring counties for work.

The German-Masontown Library was opened in 1965, the same year the Masontown Sentinel replaced the Klondike Bulletin weekly. These improvements preceded the downtown renewal project of the seventies, which brought about among other improvements, new banking facilities for Masontown's hard working population.

Main Street looking south from Church Street, early 1900's. The Altman Hotel was built by Jonathan Sterling around 1847, a few years before he built the Le Roy. It was origininally known as The Sterling House.

Another view of Main Street showing Ben Wolkoff's Department Store on the corner. Connell's Drug Store, the oldest business in Masontown, is the fourth building from the corner. The building on the right of Connell's housed a pool room and bowling alley on the second floor.

Main Street looking north, early 1900's, sometime before Main Street was paved in 1914. The Masonic Building is the first building on the left. The Le Roy Hotel is the first building on the right. The next building was the site of the Post Office of this era.

A later picture of the same view, showing Alex Mack's store on then left, followed by a barber shop, H. C. Smith's Hardware, and a watch shop. The tall building is the Masonic Building, built in 1903.

Main Street looking north from Cross Avenue, 1920's. Girard Tailors on the left, followed by the Rex Theatre. The tailors opened in 1926. The last building on the left on this block is the New Mason Hotel, built in 1910.

Main Street looking south. The drug store on the corner was owned by Randall Yeagle's father. The Atlantic and Pacific Tea Company now occupied the next building, followed by a Tom's Palace. A pool hall was located on the second floor of the next building, followed by Connell's Drug Store, and the S. J. Franklin Store. Notice the streets are now brick. This was done in 1914-1916.

Main Street looking north from Cross Avenue, in the late 1920's. The first building is the Higinbotham Building, built in 1923. The next building housed a Barber Shop, followed by the S.F. Franklin store. On the other side of the tree is The Savoy Restaurant, owned by George Franks.

North Main Street showing the R.K. Wright Ford Garage and Pennzoil, now the home of Masontown Printing.

This is a picture of Masontown's street department in the early 1900's, shown dragging the streets in front of Connell's Drug Store. Legend has it that the roads were so bad at this time that a local man fell in a mud puddle and drowned before he could be rescued.

The first hotel built in Masontown, located at the corner of Main Street and Cross Avenue, now the site of Dr. Ingraham's house. The hotel was built in 1815.

This early 1900's photo shows Dr. Ingraham's house at the intersection of Main Street and Cross Avenue.

This is one of Dr. Ingraham's first touring cars, shown parked on the unpaved Main Street in front of his house.

A view of inside Franklin's Furniture Store. Jake Franklin, the owner is on the left, his brother Izzy on the right.

This 1930 photo shows the building that was occupied by the Girard-Blassotti Clothing Store, O. Girard Tailors, and Dr. F. K. Wells, physician. The building on the right was the C. G. Deffenbaugh Hardware Store.

The First National Bank of Masontown was organized May 12, 1900, and opened its doors for business on July 16, 1900. It was the first bank in Fayette County to organize under the new banking act of Congress with a capital stock issue of $25,000. Alexander Mack was the first president. Among the members of the board of directors were Samuel Minor Gray and John C. Neff. David Ross Anderson was elected cashier at the board meeting May 23.

Repercussions from the market crash of 1929 began to be felt early in the thirties. The real blow hit Masontown when the First National Bank, which had absorbed the Masontown National Bank, closed its doors on April 17, 1931, tying up almost $2,000,000 in deposits.

On May 15, 1935, the New Second National Bank opened its doors for business and from that time a gradual improvement in business conditions continued until things again reached about normal about 1940.

This building shows the First National Bank on Main Street. The bank was organized in 1900, and was destroyed in the Great Fire of 1909.

This is the First National Bank Building, built in 1911 at the site of the building that was destroyed by the fire. This is now the site of the U.M.W.A.

Alex Mack, first president of First National Bank. He was born in 1834, and died in 1916.

The picture show the block that burned in 1909. The first building on the left was the First National Bank. The entire block was destroyed. Arson was said to be the cause of the fire which started in the rear second floor of Miller's Clothing Store. Louis Miller and his clerk, Aaron Rodney were arrested.

This view shows the block looking south. Visible are the ruins of the Altman Hotel, where the fire is said to have been deliberately set. The buildings lost in the fire were The Altman Hotel, Charlie Sangston's frame building, Frank Madas' Meat Market, Ray Anderson's Building, Jesse Sterling's Grocery Store, and the First National Bank. Notice the then undeveloped Cannon Hill in the background.

Prior to indoor motion pictures, movie pictures were shown in a tent by Charle Hartwick. He opened August 26, 1906. Admission for adults was 50¢ and children was 15¢.

The Rex Theatre was built in 1912, and was remodeled and enlarged in 1920. The feature movie for the Saturday this photo was taken featured Alice Joyce and Guy Coombs in "The Face of The Madonna."

The New Mason Hotel was built after the 1910 fire to replace the Altman Hotel. It is said that the first and only jukebox in town was in the lobby of this hotel. The hotel was run by R. B. Hays.

This is the inside of "Uncle" Rube Rhoades Store, located on Main Street, approximately across from what is now the Masontown Sentinel and Masontown Printing Offices. He opened at the Altman Hotel in 1888.

This is the inside of the Franklin Department Store, located on Main Street in Masontown. The person on the right is Izzy Franklin.

This early picture of the Le Roy Hotel, on the corner of Main and Church, shows the Le Roy Hotel Bar, The Hague Pharmacy, and The Masontown National Bank. Young boys played basketball in the second floor hall because they had no where else to play.

The first bus line in Masontown was owned by R. K. Wright, Thomas A. Hoover, and W. D. Lewis. Pictured with the bus in front of the Le Roy Hotel Entrance are Oliver C. Smith, E. W. Sterling, James Hague, George Fink, Lewis Hague, Abe Walters, W. D. Lewis, and Harry Neff.

Inside the bar at the Le Roy Hotel.

LeRoy Bowling Alley	LeROY PHARMACY	LeROY POOL ROOM
	Masontown, Pa.	JOE PETRATUS
Keep Your Girlish Figure		Masontown, Pa.
	WE ARE ALWAYS AT YOUR SERVICE.	
TRY BOWLING		ONE OF YOUR BROTHER FIREMEN
Masontown, Pa.	COUNTY FIREMEN	

Activity at an opening sale on Main Street in the early 1900's.

A group waiting for the bus ride to Ronco in front of the Hague Pharmacy in the Le Roy Hotel in 1914, Bill and Mary Ann Lewis seen second and third from front right. The Hague Pharmacy was established in 1910. The chains on the bus were needed for the muddy trek to Ronco.

This is a later picture of the Le Roy Hotel in the thirties. The corner that was once the hotel bar now houses the Masontown National Bank, known as the "Bank With The Clock". Other businesses in the building were a drug store, a barber shop, and a bowling alley and billiard hall in the basement.

Shortly after midnight July 12, 1973, fire destroyed the Le Roy Hotel Building. Businesses destroyed in the $600,000 fire included The Masontown Sentinel, Leroy Flowerland, Franks' Appliance, and the Ann Louise Dance Studio, along with the apartments located on the upper floors.

Also destroyed in the fire was LaRose's Restaurant and The Collins Lounge. The fire destroyed nearly a block in the center of the borough.

Flames can be seen inside the office of The Masontown Sentinel.

Reminiscent of the 1909 fire, all that remained the next day was a partial skeleton of the Le Roy.

Ben Wolkoff's Shoe Store, located on Main Street. Ben is shown behind the counter selling a pair of dress oxfords to Clarence Lowe. The other people in this photo are thought to be clerks who worked in the store.

The second post office in Masontown was located on North Main Street, north of the Le Roy Hotel, until approximately 1935. The first post office was located on South Main Street in a log cabin at the site of what is now Connell's drug store. After the Main Street site, it was moved to West Church Street, in the building which housed Herb Steinmann's printing shop. Kelli's Bakery is located there now, on the opposite side. The present post office, located on East Church Street, was dedicated in 1940.

Mr. Rachoff and Mr. Shuble, posed before the Masonic Building, the tallest building in Masontown. This building was constructed in 1903.

Provence-Lewis Whippet and Willys-Knight Dealership, located on Main Street at the present site of Royster's Garage. This building burned in the 1940's. The first car was Grandpa's 1905 Whippet. W. D. Lewis is seen standing beside the second auto in the photo, a Willy's Knight Sedan, which sold for $870.00 when this photo was taken.

A view of North Main Street looking south, showing Provence Sales, now a Pennzoil service station.

This is a view of Main Street in 1922, showing the rally held for the striking coal miners of the area.

This was the James "Peck" Rhoades and Beatrice Bise house, located at 407 North Main Street.

East Church Street looking east. The building on the left is the Le Roy Hotel Building, showing the restaurant and market in the basement. This was later the bowling alley. On the right is the office of M. H. Cloud, physician.

O. Girard's Cleaners in 1930, located on Water Street. The plant continues to operate in the same building today.

Church Street looking west from Main Street. The building on the right was Alex Mack's Store. The bell tower of The Public School can be seen in the background.

Another view looking west down Church Street from Main.

Clarence F. Lowe in Lowe's Auto Supply, which was located at 8 Church Street, from 1922 to 1942.

An early 1900's picture of the Masontown Cemetery, located on Church Street.

This store was Jack's Place, located on West Church Street. The house in the background was built by the Schiavoni family. Both were torn down to provide a parking lot for the present Vignali's Foodland.

The first greenhouse built by Frank Magalotti, on his property along River Avenue, around 1928. The business was called the West Masontown Greenhouse. The greenhouses were dismantled after the death of Frank Magalotti in 1964.

West Masontown Florist was part of West Masontown Greenhouses, owned by Frank Magalotti. 1948.

This 1922 photo shows John Washco at the Washco Auto Repair Shop, located on River Avenue at the site of the present Masontown Borough Equipment Building. The tow truck was a Hudson automobile converted for his towing business. This car was commonly used for this because of its large powerful engine.

Washington Street looking north from Church Street.

Another view of Washington Street looking north.

A view of Masontown and E. W. Sterling's farm.

This picture shows the street car at Harvey Avenue, Masontown. The businesses on the right were Burchianti's Grocery, Vignali's Grocery, and Dolfi's Nite Club.

Deno Dolfi at the counter in his confectionary store, located on Harvey Avenue, 1923. Later the store was changed to Deno Dolfi's Nite Club, and quickly became one of the most popular gathering places in Masontown.

DOLFI'S NIGHT CLUB

Harvey Avenue   Masontown, Pa.

DINE AND DANCE

Try Our Spaghetti -- The Best In Town

YOUR FAVORITE

Beer, Whiskey and Wine

SERVED TO YOU

The Masontown Fire Department in 1933. Front Row, left to right: Clarence Haines, Beckus, N.P. Provance, ?, ?, Charles Howard, Charles Harbison, first president; W.D. Lewis, first chief; Sam Rosenshine, Sam Darr, "Buck" Howard, Orville Johnson, ?. Second Row: Joe Potratus, Whitey Howard, Van Lowe, ?, Josephus Bowers, Ed McGill, Tom Wright, ? Bice, Andy Manchus, R.K. Wright, Lloyd Wright, ? Frank Kaprive. Third Row: ?, ?, Pete Medved, Theodore Mikolowsky, James Smith, Feet Provance, ?, ?, Harry Boyce. Fourth Row: R.P. Wright, ?, David Honsaker, Bill Ambrose, John Ralston, ? Kelly, A.C. "Flick" Smith.

A Brief History of The Masontown Volunteer Fire Department
As written By W.D. Lewis - late 1940's

The Masontown Volunteer Fire Department, Inc. was organized in the month of February 1924.

A meeting of the citizens of Masontown was called by the Burgess William D. Lewis for the purpose of organizing a Fire Department. The meeting was very well attended, and the plan was unanimously approved. It was decided to call a second meeting the following week and to invite Fire Chief George Litman, Alderman William McClelland and Attorney William J. Sangston of Uniontown to give advice as to the proper procedure of organizing. This second meeting proved to be very successful in as much as the organization was effected and the following officers elected: President, Charles N. Harbison; Vice President, Charles H. Howard; Secretary, Claude Mechus; Treasurer, Samuel Rosenshein; Chief, William D. Lewis and Assistant Chief, Benjamin R. Lardin. It was also decided at this meeting to apply for a charter. Then the question of finance was settled by appointing the Chief, William D. Lewis, as chairman of the financing committee to solicit funds to purchase the proper equipment for the fighting of fires. Chief Lewis, assisted by Chief of Police Owen V. Meighan, solicited the citizens of Masontown Borough and vicinity, who were back of the movement, for one hundred dollar subscriptions. Mr. R. K. Wright was the first subscriber to head the list for $100.00

The charter, which was secured for the Department by Attorney W. J. Sangston, Jr., a former resident of Masontown, was presented to the Department without any charge by Mr. Sangston. The Charter was dated March 4, 1924, and was signed by President Judge of Fayette County, J. Q. Van Swearingen at the first meeting of the organization in March. A number of new members were added to the roll and a by-laws committee was appointed. The committee was composed of the following members: William D. Lewis, E. F. Duncombe, and Ben Wolkoff. The question of purchasing a Fire Truck was the next order of business, and it was decided to purchase a Dodge Chassis from the Howard and Lawellen Agency of Masontown, and to have the chassis equipped with a pump, hose body, chemical tanks and all other necessary equipment for the fighting of fires. The truck was delivered and accepted by the department in August, 1924. The same month the truck was delivered, we held our first carnival or street fair. The affair proved very successful. With the proceeds of the street fair and the subscriptions received, the department paid for the fire truck - approximately $5500.00 and $550.00 for a Federal electric siren, which is still in use. Also purchased were rubber coats, boots, fire hose and other equipment. This was all accomplished in approximately seven months from the time the organization was effected.

The organization continued to grow and was very successful in combating some very serious fires in Masontown and surrounding territory. In August 1926, the department purchased the second fire truck, 1750 gallon Seagrave pumper, costing $12,500.00. The Masontown Volunteer Fire Department was the first department in Fayette County to own two pumping fire trucks. In 1940, a squad car with a 350 gallon pump was purchased for $5500.00. The Masontown Volunteer Fire Department is also equipped with an E & J Resuscitator-Inhalator-Aspirator, costing $650.00 which has many uses, such as reviving victims drowning, asphyxiation, electric shock and many other uses.

The Masontown Volunteer Fire Department has recently purchased a plot of ground on Washington Street, for which they paid $4500.00 It is the desire of the department to erect a building on the ground to house the equipment and provide a meeting place for the department. The department at the present time owns equipment valued at approximately $25,000.00 and has a very substantial bank account. The present officers of the Masontown Volunteer Fire Department are the following:

President, N.P. Provence; Vice President, W.D. Lewis, Sr.; Secretary, B.W. Sterling; Treasurer, R.P. Wright; Chief, Earl Erhard; Asst. Chief, S. H. Darr; 1st Lieutenant, William Lardin, Jr.; 2nd Lieutenand, Herbert James.

Charles H. Howard, proudly standing with the Masontown Fire Department's first fire truck, a 1924 Dodge, purchased in August, 1924.

Masontown's first fire truck, shown shortly after its acquisition in 1924.

Bill Lewis and H. Soxman, sitting in the second fire truck acquired by the Department in 1926. It was a 750 gallon Seagrave Pumper.

Masontown Volunteer Fire Department's squad car at the Firemen's Convention Parade in August, 1946, in Vandergrift, Pennsylvania.

Fire Department members marching in the Firemen's Convention Parade.

Bill Lewis supervising the construction of the Masontown Volunteer Fire Department Building, 1950.

The first Public School in Masontown was built in the early 1870's on a site donated by Josiah S. Allebaugh. Classes were held there until 1916.

A new school building was completed on Church Street in 1918. Shortly after its completion, a third story with four rooms was added. In 1929, a new wing for high school students was constructed along Washington Street.

The Jacobs Evangelical Lutheran Church was established in 1773. The original meeting house was built in 1790. It was a log cabin, built for educational and religious purposes. The church was named for Jacob Frank, who donated the land for the church. The present church, shown here, was built in 1846, and remodeled and enlarged in 1886. This is the oldest church in Fayette County.

The Masontown Synagogue, erected in 1924. This building is now the site of the German-Masontown Public Library.

In 1883, John and Elizabeth Sterling held revival services in the old brick M.C. Church. Rev. A. J. Sterling was soon elected pastor of this new group, and a church was built and dedicated September 13, 1885, as the Masontown Brethren Church.

The All Saints Church was organized in 1908, with 100 Catholic families in the Masontown area. The cornerstone for their building was laid on September 26, 1909. The new church was dedicated April 24, 1910. Reverend Francis J. Kolb, L.L.D. was the first pastor. This photo shows the church and school soon after its completion.

A front view of All Saints Church, around 1911.

All Saints Church, a few years after its construction, with landscaping completed. This picture was taken from the vacant lot where the Yoney Funeral Home Building now stands. The garage west of the church was Kaas Garage. Notice the area to the left of the school is sparsely populated at this time.

Former Pastors of All Saints Church
Rev. Fr. Francis J. Kolb
Rev. Fr. Andrew J. King
Rev. Fr. William J. Donnerbauer
Msgr. Andrew J. Schneider
Rev. Fr. Andrew J. Charnoki
Rev. Fr. Leonard Stacoviak

First Church Committee — 1908
Thomas Connell, Secretary
John Payton • J. W. Campbell
Patrick Mullen • Francis Rocks
P. Callaghan • John Smith
L. B. Callaghan • Patrick Walsh
Bryan McGinty • James McKenna
John Walsh

The Very Rev. Francis J. Kolb, L.L.D.

All Saints School and Sisters Home. The Parochial School opened in 1911.

Kolb Memorial High School, opened in 1929.

The Pal's Club was organized in 1932 in this building owned by the Hillman Coal and Coke Company.

Since their beginning, the Pal's Club of Masontown (Bessemer), has steadily prospered. In 1932 they met in a small building owned by the Hillman Coal and Coke Company. Mr. D. R. DePriest worked for the company and it was under his supervision that the fraternal organization began.

In order to acquire the use of the building, founding members were to study mining, mine rescue, and first aid, in addition to their social and sporting activities.

It was George Mehalovich who suggested the name "Pal's Club" as the men came together through strong bonds of friendship. Through the years the Pal's have proven their dedication to the community in numerous ways such as forming sport teams and helping to erect an Honor Roll for local soldiers after World War II.

After eleven years in the mine shack, the Pal's Club bought six acres from the Hillman Company in 1943. The Club was chartered in 1946 and licensed in 1949. In 1950 they purchased ten acres and built a new athletic field.

From their first football game on Thanksgiving Day in 1943, the Pal's Club formed teams to be proud of. That first game was held in McClellandtown. They beat the Glassport Odds 13-0 before a crowd of 2000 fans. After two seasons of organized football, softball and baseball teams were formed with much success. Under the management of John Biskup, Pal's Club Baseball Teams in the County League won both the regular seasons of 1961, 1962, and 1963 and the County Championship.

In 1957 the club bought the Bessemer School Building and the four lots there were donated by the Hillman firm. They remodeled it into a Community Center. Then in 1980, The Pal's Club, after years of strife, moved into their new home. They have a large social room, bar, and fully equipped kitchen and year after year they pass out Christmas Treats to children of members, in the true Pal's Club tradition.

D. R. "Bob" DePriest, Pal's Club Founder

1933 OLD CLUB ROOM — Left to Right: John Jesso, Jr., John Nestar, Andy Mrazek, William, Lou, and Steve Jesso, Jerry Burchianti.

PALS CLUB OFFICERS IN 1948 — Head of Table, Melvin Smargie, President. Left side of table, front to back: Joe Grassi, Secretary; Albert Jesso, Librarian; Andrew Mrazek, Trustee; Stephen Jesso, Trustee. Right side, Front to back: Rubeh Dunham, George Mehalovich, George Lucas, Lou Jesso, Earnest Raubaugh, all trustees.

At one time the club had tennis courts, but found it impossible to maintain them. They were replaced by a playground with horseshoe pits, and soccer and basketball courts.

Pals Club tennis players in the good old days.

Socializing at the old club house.

A Pal's Club Picnic, 1934.

Pal's Club Championship Team — 1961. Front row, left to right: Bob Messich, Tom Croftcheck, Ed Hercik, Bat boy George Biskup, Bob Korcheck, Bill Marovic. Second row: Dick Cole, Bill Jones, Lefty Rodosovich, Doc Franks, Joe Hatella, Fred Answine. Third row: Mike Swetz, Tony Labis, John Biskup, Manager; Joe Lucocic, Joe Geran, Yush Messich, Andy Biskup, Bob Brooks, Steve Biskup, Metro Swetz. Absent when photo was taken was Ed Tekavec.

1950 ALL STAR GAME — Left to right: John Lozar, George Yasenosky, Joe Crackovich, and William (Bush) Burke.

The Bridge across the Monongahela River, built 1925-1926. This bridge was originially opened as a toll bridge. The toll was collected on the Greene County side. The railroad tunnel gave access to Mount Sterling.

Looking at the bridge from the tracks in Mount Sterling. Left to right: Harold Rogers, Rex Rogers and George Bierbower.

Ferry at Masontown Bridge. B. E. (Kopy) Kaprive, Jr. driving the touring car with his father in the back seat. Service was discontinued in 1927.

Railroad Station at Mount Sterling, 1920's.

Steam locomotive approaching Mount Sterling.

Men assembling cars for Bill Lewis' Touring Service that ran from Masontown to Ronco. The cars arrived in parts on the train at Mount Sterling, and were assembled at the station.

Workers taking a break during the assembly process.

Masontown Glass Factory at Mount Sterling in 1908. The factory employed approximately 400 men. It burnt April 18, 1930.

Masontown Brewery and Glass Factory at Mount Sterling in 1910. The brewery was built in 1903 and opened in 1904. It was a very successful operation until the 18th Amendment was passed.

Masontown Brewing Company, Mount Sterling.

Taking a break and having a brew with man's best friend are Joe Ferary, Sr. and M. Gardner, 1920.

Bill Lewis ran a touring service between Masontown and Ronco. This photo shows the cars on the dirt road between the two towns.

When early motorists broke down along the road, they had no AAA to call. This often created a major traffic jam. The car on the right is a Model T Ford roadster.

This 1910 photo shows a Ford Model T touring, that was the first auto purchased for the touring service.

Driving through Ronco in 1915. The car Lewis is driving is a thought to be a Model T, perhaps with a custom grill.

This is a Model T Ford in front of Lewis's garage in Ronco.

These two automobiles are thought to be air-cooled Franklins, also owned by Bill Lewis, shown parked in Ronco.

Smith and Lewis Transfer

Two of the Bill Lewis' daughters posing in the back of their father's transfer truck.

Wright's Store in Ronco. Dick and Debbie Wright in car. Lloyd perferred the horse.

Lewis and Wright Home in Ronco.

Grandma Lloyd with daughters Margaret and Mary Louis doing needle point.

Eleanor Lewis and Mary, the wash woman at the Lewis House in Ronco in the early 1900's.

Ronco School, 1918. Dorothy Rice first row standing, fifth from right. Catherine Hoover is in the same row, fourth from right.

A meadow in Ronco. When reminiscing about this photograph, Dorothy Lewis Rice explained that even though they looked like a happy bunch, "Life was not a song". From left, Dick Wright and Family; Ruth Sterling, center with bow; Dorothy and Eleanor Lewis, front center; Mary Ann holding baby Deborah with husband Bill Lewis holding the calf; Hanson Sterling on crutches; Mrs. Hoover on the right with two unidentified children.

Yesteryear In New Geneva

There are three "mounds" built by early ancestors called the Mound Builders around New Geneva. One sits at the intersection of Routes 166 and 266. The others are near there. These mounds were used for ceremonial purposes and many bones, tools, etc. were buried there.

Albert Gallatin bought the lands of New Geneva from the estate of Colonel George Wilson for $3000.00. He named the town after his native city in Switzerland and signed the charter October 31, 1797. That same year Gallatin and Company built a glass plant along Georges Creek. They were in business at least 12 years shipping large loads of glassware and hollow ware to Pittsburgh and Kentucky. Two years later he and partner, Melchoir Baker organized a gun manufacturer. They made muskets, broad swords, and other weapons for the state and federal governments.

A bird's eye view of New Geneva.

Another view of New Geneva, showing the covered bridge. One can see the location of the pottery kiln on the right side of the picture.

This picture shows the stone church and honor roll, located in New Geneva.

Taking a break from the reconstruction of Route 166 in New Geneva, sometime in the late 1920's.

A gathering of workers and children at the New Geneva Pottery.

Workers posing for the photographer at the kiln in New Geneva, about 1907.

Norrey the potter throwing a piece of stoneware. Notice the foot-operated kickwheel to turn the pot.

Inside the New Geneva Pottery, installing handles on the jugs before they were placed in the kiln to be fired.

A flat boat used to transport New Geneva Pottery down the Monongahela River to Pittsburgh and West. Left to right: A. Mackinson, F. Neal, L. Rumble.

Yesteryear With Albert Gallatin at Friendship Hill

Albert Gallatin was born January 29, 1761 in Geneva, Switzerland. Orphaned at the age of nine, he graduated from the Academy of Geneva in 1779 and traveled to Massachusetts in 1780.

Albert Gallatin

From 1781-83 he operated a store in Macias, Maine, tutored French at Harvard, worked as interpreter and companion for Savary de Voucouion of Lyons firm and acquired part interest in land in western Pennsylvania.

During the next two years he delved into land speculation in Virginia, Pennsylvania, and Ohio, purchasing Friendship Hill in 1786. During the next seven years he constructed his residence on Friendship Hill.

Among Gallatin's political achievements are three consecutive one-year terms in the PA legislature, being elected and expelled from the Senate, acting as a mediator to help calm the Whiskey Rebellion, serving as Secretary of the Treasury under Presidents Jefferson and Madison, and helping to negotiate and sign the Treaty of Ghent, putting an end to the war of 1812.

Toward the end of his term as U.S. Minister to France from 1816-23, he had his Friendship Hill residence enlarged. In 1832 he sold the property to Albin Mellier, Jr.

After going through many hands, Friendship Hill was sold to the United States Government December 31, 1979. The site contains 661.44 acres. The estate has been preserved to remember Gallatin's many contributions to the political, financial and diplomatic development of the United States. The home served as a retreat. He was visited there by Lafayette on May 27, 1825.

Gallatin later settled in New York, where he became a bank president.

Front view of Friendship Hill

Rear view of Friendship Hill

Grave of Sophia Allegre, first wife of Albert Gallatin at Friendship Hill.

Friendship Hill's lookout overlooking the Monongahela River

The following three pages show some of the rooms and furnishings inside Friendship Hill, from the Albert Gallatin era.

Original dining room, 1789.

State dining room.

Drawing room

LaFayette Room

Bedroom

Bedroom

Yesteryear in Bessemer

The Bessemer Coke Company was the largest independent plant in the new Klondike Region in 1902. Of it's 750 acres of coal, 730 acres were self draining. Bessemer lies within ½ mile of Masontown and was along the South West Pennsylvania Railroad. In an article in a Special Edition of The Genius of Liberty (Uniontown newspaper) called "Illustrated Industrial Edition of Masontown, Pennsylvania", it states that they presently (April 1902) had 303 ovens in operation and were building 200 more.

The quality of the coke was said to be superior for both blast furnaces nad foundry purposes. The Bessemer Coke Company started only a few years before this with a mere 100 ovens throughout their numerous plants, several of which were in Westmoreland County.

Coke is a soft coal that has had the gases expelled in a hot, enclosed. At the turn of the century cokemaking ranked as one of the great industries of the United States, revolutionizing the iron and steel trade world wide. It was coke that made Pittsburgh the iron capital of the country.

You must have the right kind of coal and the right kind of water to make coke. Coke ovens stretched out from the shaft top of coal mines on either side of the railroad tracks. They were built close together and look like a wall of masonary with low arched windows. These are the oven doors. A narrow-guage track runs over the bank of ovens carrying small dump cars called "larries". These carry the coal from the shaft top to the oven. Mules and horses - even cattle - wer eused to pull these cars before locomotives and electricity. The horses and wagons were guided by a "driver". The driver was paid by the wagon load, each holding about 50 bushel. The company supplied each driver with a horse. When the man was not working, the horse rested, too.

The "Push Ovens" at Bessemer.

Wagon Number One Hundred
A Story For Miners by Robert C. McClelland
Taken From Masontown, Pennsylvania and Its Environs

Old timers will remember the patch at Bessemer No. 1, in the hollow south of Masontown, about half a mile above Ifield Station. It was a somewhat bedraggled place, scarcely fit, in some respects, for human habitation; but it seemed comfortable enough for Havey "Pickle Nose" Leonard, Tucker Hughes, and fifty other miners. It was also the home of Mike, the ill-fated hero of the present story. Though he did not always feel elevated in spirit, Mike was fairly comfortable there, for his home was close to the lamp house and manway - an important consideration on cold mornings or in the afternoon, after a hard day's work. Mike didn't complain: he just dug coal, "on the solid". He was an expert "rib man".

On the morning of our present interest, Mike walked down the hill as usual, at 5:50 o'clock, with dinner bucket in hand, and the picks which he had brought out for sharpening on the previous afternoon. Without much exchange of conversation, he checked in, picked up his safety lamp, and directed his steps to the manway which opened in the hill a few hundred yards away. Then, in five minutes or so, he turned right on the main haulage and proceeded a half-mile to his place of labor. Just the ordinary course of events - but this time with a difference.

For some who read these pages but have forgotten, it may be well to recall that the Provins Main Dip entries began at Number Five Flat switch, from which point they were driven westward to the Gray's Landing line, with Five, Six, Seven and Eight Face Flats on the left, and Flats A, B, C, D, and E on the right. The whole large section was a "rib line" on both sides, that is, the entries had been driven to the boundary and the pillars were being "pulled back". Hazardous work for all concerned, it was, but economically productive because of the quicker and cheaper output. Miners at the face, too, liked to work on the "retreat", where ribs and stumps were often crushed by the weight of hundreds of feet of disturbed rock, with correspondingly easier digging. Such was the case in Mike's place, in E Flat, on the right gob line. And Mike has prospered there in recent weeks.

Our chief character, on the morning concerned, was occupied with two main considerations. First, although approaching middle age, he had some years earlier imported a young wife from Slavic Europe, and she had blessed him with five children in quick succession. Consequently, every wagon loaded represented a welcome addition to the family exchequer, especially since the rising prices of war days had imposed a strain. Growing families mean high grocery bills, and increasing expenditures for clothing, medicine, and numerous other things incident to housekeeping. Every dollar counted much in a miner's life.

Second, a matter of much importance in this distant narrative, at the beginning of the pay period, two weeks earlier, the company had announced a raise of twelve cents per two-ton wagon, adjusting the price from fifty-four to sixty-six cents. Mike had loaded ninety-one wagons during the past thirteen days, and today, the last day of the period, he was determined to load the hundredth wagon before nightfall. An excellent prospect, $66.00 for a payday, more than Mike had ever received!

All went well until shortly after noon. Mike had loaded wagon number ninety-seven and was working on another. Only two more to go after this and the day would end beautifully! The stump which he pounded was now reduced to a small compass and the strata above were cracking and groaning ominously. The section foreman came by for his usual second visit and told Mike to finish the wagon, call the driver immediately, remove his tools, and summon the rib boss to set the break-row and make the fall; that is, to remove the track and all the posts and timbers that could be retrieved before the place should be obliterated by thousands of ton or rock and rubble. Again, the usual procedure.

But Mike debated the matter: only two to go now, and he was accustomed to uneasy rock and creaking timbers. he was determined to load Number One Hundred. The foreman wouldn't know the difference, so why talk to the driver or the rib boss? Surely there were four tons more in that stump: it appeared still to be fairly strong . . . Thus Mike won the debate with himself and proceeded to work on wagon number ninety-nine. Another foreman came by, gave Mike the same instructions which he had had an hour before, and went on his way. But Mike debated again - and started work on Wagon Number One Hundred.

The rock above was more uneasy now: cracks had developed here and there, and the warning odor of petroleum permeated the working place. Two or three timbers gave way under the enormous pull of gravity, and several posts bent as though they must soon split apart. The stump, on which Mike hammered with quickened strokes of the pick, seemed to give up the struggle, as was made evident by the crushed coal which fell from time to time even while Mike was wielding the shovel. Only a half-hour more and number one hundred would be recorded in the ledger at the office. The healthiest pay that Mike had ever received. . .

Bill, the driver, brought his trip up the heading and prepared to pull the loads from the miner's places, then to replace them with empties. Bill was anticipating an evening on the town, more than glad to reflect that things had gone well that day and that he might be done his work earlier than the usual hour. Old Doc, the horse, trudged along at his usual plodding speed, tired at this point from seven hours of heavy labor. He too was dreaming, of a comfortable stall in the barn outside the mine, and of a feed box filled with oats - his ordinary pay for a day of laboriuos service. It was that quiet hour in the depths of the earth when, despite the darkness, day seemed to be approaching its close. It was mid-afternoon.

Suddenly the rattling of wheels on the iron rails, the clanking of the tail chain, and the heavy sound of Doc's footsteps were lost in the roar of a terrific crash. The bottom of the passage way and walls shook as though assailed by a gigantic explosion. A blast of displaced air swept over horse and driver - air from Mike's place just ahead. Then, after some seconds of deafening collapse from above, a kind of silence prevailed, broken only by the rattle of small fragments that trickled down around the edges of the mass that had disintegrated Mike's place of labor. Wagon Number 100 was lost under countless tons of rock, slate, and primeval debris.

Mike was lost, too. A rescue gang extracted the corpse on the next afternoon, after twenty-four hours of dangerous and exhausting effort. Herb Johnson had another client, mourned by a widow and five children, their hopes and livelihood gone together with the hundredth wagon, which was not recovered. It is still enveloped by broken rock in the E-Flat gob, several hundred feet below one of Silas Provin's cornfields.

The coke ovens at Bessemer.

The entrance of the Bessemer Mine.

On the left is the power house at the Bessemer Mine. The tipple is on the right.

The Office Staff at the Bessemer Mine included Charles Baxter, Pearl Wimer, Cliff Whetzel, Ray Martin and Cal Martin.

Si Piper and Bill King worked in the Blacksmith Shop at the Bessemer Mine.

An honest day's work at the Bessemer Coke Yard. Tom Skiles on the right.

Taking a much needed break for the photographer were these early workers.

Automation comes to the Bessemer Coke Yard.

Loading coal into the railroad cars for transportation is a much easier job now. The last coke was drawn in May of 1952 from Bessemer No. 2, marking over 50 years of operation at that plant.

A mine team first aid competition at the Leckrone Ball Field. The mine tipple is shown on the left of the picture; the bridge visible in the background was a railroad bridge; and the coke ovens are seen from the center to the right of this photo.

Early mine cars at the Leckrone mine.

Accidents happened frequently in the early years of mining. This picture at Leckrone shows a wrecked runaway mine car.

Can't Find A Cause For The Big Explosion. That was the headline of the article in The Daily Standard of Uniontown on August 2, 1917, concerning the Leckrone plant. Six boilers at H. C. Frick's Coke Company there had blown up suspending the plant's operations entirely. According to the story, there were three deaths: Joseph Chefchek (ash wheeler), Frederick Henning (fireman), and Tony Peader (fireman in boiler plant). Joseph Bush was in very serious condition with internal injuries.

The three victims had been sitting against the wall of the power house, 100 feet from the boiler room when the big steam generators let go. Investigators were unsure of the cause, suspecting the possibility of an outside agency. They believed that cold water was forced into the pipes which caused the safety warning whistle to fail.

Mrs. Mary Amrick was hanging out clothes with her daughter 200 yards away and was struck by flying brick and debris, as was Charles Skiles, who was walking along the railroad track.

Officials concluded that, since only employees were there at the time, the disaster was an accident. The 200 men working below the plant quickly evacuated while Drs. E. R. Ingram, D. H. Sangston, J. Holmes Sangston, S. E. Peters, John J. Mechem and John Messmore quickly came to their aid along with the Uniontown Hospital ambulance. Rescue teams from Leckrone and Leisenring No. 2 plants recovered the remains which were buried under tons of brick.

Taking a break from the clean-up of the boiler explosion at the Leckrone Mine.

Clean-up crew at the explosion, Kopy Kaprive in the white shirt.

This was the scene on August 18th, 1926, during the Safety First Dinner of the Leckrone Mine.

Safety First Dinner at Leckrone. At the far end of the table was Steve Hanigosky; Frank Miller was at this end. On the left side, front to back, were Walter Lockwood, Clyde Lutton, Patty Mullen, Charles McDerrmont, B. C. Bell, Ralph Sherrick, Clyde Sechler, and W. J. Culleton. On the right side were Charles Brown, Russ McIntyre, A. B. Gault, Sam Dennisson, Bill Ambrose, Harry Millword, and Mike Girod.

The Leckrone Union Supply Company Department delivery at the Leckrone Ball Field in the 1920's. The tipple can be seen in the background on the right, and mining cars are seen on the tracks hauling coal from the mine.

Play Ball!! at the Leckrone Ball Field in the 1920's. The tipple and coke ovens can be seen in the background on the left.

The Brady House located at Gallatin on Route 166, south of Masontown.

Surveying the damage after the mine explosion at Rocks Works.

Mine explosions caused much destruction, as is evident in this photo of Rocks Works.

Sunshine in June, 1913, after the explosion.

Lamberton had no ball field, but this failed to stop America's favorite past time, as shown by the turnout at the mine located there.

Yesteryear In Palmer

H. C. Frick Company bought the 1,800 acres of coal land that was the Palmer Mine in 1908. By 1957, the last of the coal was mined out and life as Palmer residents knew it, changed drastically.

The Palmer Dock and Harbor were built in 1917 and 1918 on the Monongahela River. Entries driven through Palmer territory were used to move coal by rail from the inland mines in Ralph, Filbert, Buffington, Footedale, and Lambert. Transporting by underground rail was a quick and inexpensive way to haul the coal to the river tipple. From there it was shipped by barge to the by-product coke plant in Clarion. In 1928, a belt conveyor system replaced this underground rail transportation. From 1918-1928 about 33 million tons were shipped by underground rail. From 1929-1957, about 65 million tons of coal had been delivered to the Palmer River Dock over the conveyor for shipment.

This picture of the mine tipple at Palmer was taken before the docks were constructed in 1917 and 1918.

View of the Palmer Mine and patch, early 1900's.

The Palmer Community Band entertained residents of its community for many years. In the first row, left to right, are Ralph and Louis Bill, John Logston, Ben Watson, Joseph Angle, Ingraham Riffle and Ed Fisher. Second row: Harry Rose, George Drews, Sam Bill, Harry Welsh, Regis Maher, Ted Bliss, Joseph Zacovic, Jacob Podwyski, Frank Wright and Henry Drews. Third Row: John Pluto, Edward Rumanyek, Roy Hoon, Andrew Banuas, Wiley Riffle, Charles Hughes, Charles Lewis, Mike Pavlik, Les Walker, Furd Shaffer, Hiram Fike and Ralph Artis.

Palmer Mine also had its baseball team, and the 1925 team is shown here. Standing, left to right, are Charles Sabo, Paul Chuey, William Miller, Joe Yanosik, Robert Hoop, Lee Burkey, Roy Hoon, Charles Provance, Calvin Masters, and James Welsh, manager. Seated is Harry Welsh, mascot.

Yesteryear In McClellandtown

The village was founded by William McClelland who died there at the age of 82 July 12, 1815.

In 1882, McClellandtown had a post office, two stores, three blacksmith shops, two wagon makers, two saddlers, a buggy shop, and several carpenters, millwrights, and shoemakers. Many homes were being built then.

In Robert C. McClelland's book, Masontown, Pennsylvania and It's Environs - A Contribution to their History, he states that he and friends uncovered a mound built by the ancient mound builders in McClellandtown. It had a hard clay core and showed evidence of fire on two levels. It was 30 feet in diameter at its base and 20 feet in height.

B. S. Newcomer family and home in McClellandtown.

McClellandtown's skyscraper, the A. E. Moser and Company General Store.

This late 1800's photograph shows the building housing a store, post office, and telephone office.

This early 1900's photo shows the inside of the general store in Puritan, just over the hill from McClellandtown.

Yesteryear in Footedale

A view of Footedale from the top of the mine tipple. Seen on the left is the mine stable.

This photo, also from the top of the tipple, shows another view of Footedale. On the right is the Footedale School. The company store and St. Thomas Church can be seen in the background.

This photo shows the mine stable and horses in Footedale.

The large boss's house at Footedale.

This picture shows the shanty at Footedale Mine where Scott Messenger was stable boss from 1924-29.

A Sunday gathering at Charles Marshall's garden in the Footedale patch.

Yesteryear In New Salem

In 1799 David Arnold bought the village property area then known as "Stuffle's Policy". He laid out a town of sixty lots and named it New Salem. At this time a grist mill owned by James Thompson was the main business there but soon Solomon Hickman opened a tavern (1802) and his father became the village doctor. Soon a store and two blacksmiths went into business.

New Salem was known as "Muttontown" because many stolen sheep were traced there. It acquired a reputation as a place filled with drunks, gambling, and thieves until a temperance society was formed in 1835 protesting the trafficking of whiskey. In 1843 the last tavern closed it's doors, bringing about a wholesome environment.

Main Street, New Salem, Pennsylvania, in the early 1900's.

The intersection of Main and Mill Streets, New Salem, the First National Bank on the right.

Briscoe's Marathon, New Salem, May 15, 1909.

The Hotel Anderson, Main Street, New Salem.

The First National Bank, corner of Main and Mill Streets, New Salem, now the site of Integra Bank. This photo is from the late 1920's.

The S. O. McCormick Grain Mill, 1909. Pictured are Sam O. McCormick, George E. McCormick, and son Eugene. In the doorway is Jesse B. McCormick.

The Greek Catholic Church, New Salem, 1910.

Inside the Greek Catholic Church, 1910.

The Public School, now the site of the New Salem Volunteer Fire Department on Mill Street.

Students at St. Procopius Parochial School.

Like most other local towns at the turn of the century, New Salem also had its own community band. Front row left to right: Ralph Funk, Brice Beal, Ewing Jeffries, William Molton, William Frost, Ed Hackney, Wade Moss, Sylvester Walters, Park Coffman. Top row: Charley Roderick and son Carl, Merl Russel, Herman Russell, Bob Seaton, Glenn Gribble, Newton Hibbs, Jonah M. Dearth.

New Salem also had its community baseball team. Some of the people pictured here in this 1880's photo are Charlie McCombs, front row, first from left; Bill Cropp, back row, third from left; Patty Dorsey, sixth from left, Mr. Cropp.

Flu epidemic of 1918 took this New Salem family to an early grave. Clark B. Dearth with hat on far left. Paul Tuit driving the hearse.

This 1930's photo shows the mine at Filbert.

Miners entering shaft entrance of Filbert Mine of H. C. Frick Coke, Co., Fairbanks. Note cage load of men ready to descend.

Track-type coal cutting machine in position to make side cut. E. J. Carroll, cutter, right, and W. H. Carroll, scraper, left. Photo taken in Filbert Mine.

Yesteryear People

Masontown School, Room 2, 1914.

Masontown High School, Graduating Class of 1931. Front row, left to right: Sophia (Furin) Culleton, Edward Ganoczy, Martha Barnhart, George Heid, Mary Furlick, Geno Packroni, Pauline Mixey, Mary Hanna, Hannah (Ainsley) Ruppert. Second row: Vi Sullivan, Meyer Franklin, Deborah Lewis, Sue (Haught) Organt, Thomas Johnston, Eunice (Schlitz) Huhn, Lewis Cinci, Florence (Townsend) Diamond, Herbert Simpson. Third row: Odward J. Girard, Ova Kay Hunsaker, Leroy Sterling, Virginia Anne (Lardin) Gapen.

All Saints School play, late 1930's.

A class at Bessemer School.

Bessemer Rhythmn Band, 1929. Front row, left to right: Marie Deffenbaugh, Junior Warman, Elizabeth McDowell, ?, Kathryn Johnson, Ruben Bailey, Marge Matyus, Julia Billak, Walter DeMaske, Pete Smargie, ?. Second row: Elizabeth Milnarcik, Hazel Dugan, Frances Hoist, Helen Dubroka, John Chahl, Marie Honsaker, Charles Ivan Hamilton, Anna Mae Gomer, Elizabeth Lucas, Eleanore Hower. Third row: Mary Lakatos, Harry Dayton, Elizabeth McKenna, Helen Vargo, David Johnson, Steve Nestarec, Dan Cappellini, Julia Sierzanga, Leona Kimmel, Matt Milnarcik, Sonny Sofranko.

All Saints church picnic, Leckrone Hill. Father Kolb the church's founder is seated in the center.

The men of Ronco Union Church, early 1900's. Pictured are Nick Dominick, Sam Darr, Andy Powell, Joe Lusco, Harry Kestler, Mr. McManus, Albert Sharpneck, Armal Johnston, Chas. Twyford, George Barnhart, Frank Roll, Albert Hague, Jacob Heck, Chas. Sanners, Jim Sanners, Chris Dunlap. Roy Sharpnack, Sam Grim, Dick Wright, Leslie Barnhart, Ed Marks, Mr. Gawney, Teacher A. G. Smart, Pastor C. O. Bemies.

Masontown businessmen on holiday in Gettysburg. Pictured are Tom Miller, blacksmith; Walter Blaney, feed mill; Hershal Darrall, lumberman: James Altman, painter; "Rube" Rhoades, dry good merchant; Will Howard, blacksmith; Charley McGill, worked at lumber yard; Dave Lardin, taxi driver.

A gathering at Dr. Ingraham's house, Main Street, Masontown. Pictured are Mrs. Paul Howard, Aunt Etty Allebaugh, Dr. Ingraham's mother, Ade Kail, Mrs. "Doll" Rhoades, Mrs. Alex Mack, Mrs. J. M. Howard, Mrs. G. W. Neff, Mrs. William Lardin, Mrs. Jess Hoover, Aunt Ida Sharpnack, Mrs. James Weltner, Mrs. Charles Sangston, Mrs. Emma Darrall, Mrs. Frank Conn, Mrs. Charles Walters, Mrs. O. C. Smith, Mrs. Emma Clifford, Mrs. Will Howard, Mrs. Mertie Darrall, Rev. Auld's wife, Mrs. Herb Johnston, Mrs. Sim Stillwell, Mrs. Lela Meecham, Mrs. Rube Rhoades, Mrs. Ingraham, Mrs. Charley Harbison, Mrs. Ray Anderson, Maggie Hempstead, Ivy Martin, Mrs. George McLeod.

A gathering in Masontown in the early 1900's.

Italian Ladies Circle, 1948. First row (sitting): Mrs. Angela Mocibob, Josephine Albertini, Rica Bonessa, Mary Valentine, Gina Funari, Pearl Malpezzi, Segee Righi, Marie Demolli, Genoeffa Brice, Genoeffa Cantini, Caterina Cassini. Second row: Nora Bartaroni, Antoinetta Coll, Mary Virgini, Rose DeFino, Thresa Rozzi, Mary Ann Micozzi, Teresa Frasconi, Rose Dunn, Josephine Albani, Mary Ann Mojock, Angela Organtini, Josephine Vent, Cesira Chiti, Emilia Battaglini, Ada Albani, Anna Revetta, Frances Polzen, Anna Mego, Rose Timperio, Amabile Lazembri, Frances DiNardo, Elmerinda Raqusa, Sabina Rossini. Top row: Carmela Stacy, Anna Grassi, Camilla Williams, Armida Nocenti, Sofia Carnacelli, Katy Brill, Angela Zammarelli, Luisa Ferrandi, Elvina Vicinelli, Caroline Bevilaczua, Vernada Trincia, Gertrude Schiavoni, Luisa Giamberardini, Anette Uhall, Frances Soavi, Cesira Alexander, Betty Fugazzotti, Assunata Micoli, Adeline Barchetti.

Ladies of the Italian Circle gathered after their play, "Love and Duty", November 28, 1937.

First street car in Masontown on Harvey Avenue, September 6, 1907.

The following poem was written by Everella Virginia Neff September 6, 1907, as the first street car entered Masontown.

Masontown's Old Times

Oh for the good old times,
   The pleasant days of yore
When Alex Mack taught our school,
   And John Ross kept the store
Elder Doctor Neff gave our medicine
   On a little yellow pony Jonah Arrison brought the news.
James Bradley made our footwear
   And we all wore calfskin shoes.
Aaron Walters tanned the leather
   C. T. Rhoads ran the hotel.
We burned the tallow candle
   James C. Eddington was the squire.
We cracked nuts and jokes
   As we sat around the bright coal fires.
Barney Williams was the tailor
   Elder William Schroyer made the velvet casket
Zedus Linton made the harness
   Dutch Betsey made the ryestraw basket
Denoona Howard was the cooper
   Dick Webber made the heavy wooden chair
West Altman was the painter
   And we didn't have a barber to cut the hair.
Nick Yonta made the whiskey
   And it ran as free as water in the brook
Just a dram in the harvest field,
   Is all we took.
Oh for those golden olden times
   For the stranger, large buildings, automobiles and painted signs.
   Today we throw our gates ajar
And welcome to our town
   the first street car
The sun shines bright
   And the day is one of joy and delight.
The speaking all is grand
   We are treated to fine music from the band
We gave a dinner free,
   Of roasted ox and everything good to eat.
Then at night we gave a lawn fete
   The boys from Edenborn came
And beat our boys in a baseball game
   Everybody is kindly treated to a free ride to Leckrone
And back home.
   This is a day we all shall remember
Nineteen hundred and seven, the sixth day of September.

A group of coal miners from Edenborn and Grays Landing.

The "Yellow Dogs" or strike breakers, shown outside the mine at Edenborn in 1922.

Masontown Bus Lines, 1947. Kneeling left to right: Paul Ferranti, Dominic Schiavnoi, Ray Clark, Carmine Peluso, Dr. George Yanchus. Standing: Geno Coll, unknown, Dominic Schiavoni, Jr., Joe Schiavnoi, Randolph Fast.

Carmine Appliance Company, 1945 Crosley Promotion. Left to right: Tom Javorsky, Carmine Peluso, Sr., Crossley Representive, Eugene Franks and Paul Ferranti.

Masontown Baseball Team, 1914.

Masontown Baseball Team, 1920.

Masontown Semi-Pro Team of the 1920. Van B. Lowe, Nicily (professional); Ott Schmitt, Stuffy Carroll, (pro.); Steve Yanchus, Skinny Williams, Frank Schmitt, Bill Helmick (semi-pro.); Sam Darr, Grant Bowman, Bill Doak (pro.); Bill Danley.

Bill Doak, spitball pitcher for the St. Louis Nationals and the first spitball hurler once said: "Masontown is the richest little town I was ever in."

Robert C. McClelland, in his 1962 book, Masontown and Its Environs, reminisces about the above picture. The following are some of his thoughts:

Not in a long while have I felt so keenly, almost painfully, the effects of passing time as I did last Saturday, February 10, when I stopped at Van Lowe's office to transact a few matters of business. Remembering that Van had been past years an ardent baseball man, I approached the subject of Masontown's outstanding players of an earlier era, a subject which is yet close to Van's spirit, part of a treasure house of memories. After some reminiscences, Van pointed to a picture on the wall near his desk, and there gazed forth still the members of Masontown's great team of 1920, in a picture taken at the park in West Masontown. Van himself appeared there, forty-two years younger and, one may properly remark, giving evidence of the eager, competitive nature which he brought to every game. Frank Schmidt was there, and his brother Ott. Bill Danley and Bill Doak looked only a little older than boys, as did Bill Helmick, Stuffy Carroll, and Steve Yanchus. Grant Bowman wore his usual serious expression, bringing thoughts to me of his skilled plays at second base, his "rabbit" singles into right field, just far enough to be out of reach of a first baseman but too close for the man in right field, also of Grant's slow feet - he had to hit the ball into the woods in order to reach second base. Van assured me, however, that Grant became determined one day, resolved to emulate several teammates, and hit a ball for a home run into the trees west of the diamond on the old Sterling property in West Masontown. Old timers, and near old timers, will remember the championship game against Republic which Masontown lost 1 to 0, when Stuffy Carrol lost a pitch that stirred much debate - whether Bill Doak made a wild heave or that Stuffy simply couldn't see one of Bill's "spitters". And who will not recall that the Reverend Crapper closed up the town and made us all so good on Sunday afternoons, at the same time causing the disbanding of the baseball team? How we missed our Coca-Colas, then comparatively new in the town . . . I do not recall whether we were shrived of our many sins.

Masontown Little League All-Stars, 1954 Pennsylvania State Champs. First row: B. Fronczek, M. Pscenski, A. Brugger, T. Byers, bat boy; J. Hatella, E. Verbos, G. Dunn. Second row: T. Rozzi, Manager; S. Radosevich, R. Pramuk, M. Banner, R. Albani, F. Rossini, J. Takacs, J. Manchus, J. Yakubic, M. Novasky, Assistant Manager.

Two of the German Township cheerleaders shown here rooting for the team in 1929 were Ruth Rupart and Maude Lardin.

Masontown Football Team, 1916.

German Township High School Football Team, 1924.

Eleanor and Bud Franks, working on the first edition of The Masontown Sentinel, June, 1965. The Sentinel Office was located in the Le Roy Hotel Building until the fire.

Nell and Edna Hoover, daughters of James Hoover, leave their German Township farm for a day on the town.

Betty Clark of Lamberton, shown in full riding gear, off for a afternoon drive on her 1920 Harley-Davidson.

David Ray Johnson, owner of a plumbing and heating business in Masontown for many years, driving his Maxwell, one of the early cars in Masontown, 1909.

Louis Wheeler shown here beside his truck, 1918.

A 1920 wedding for Margaret Marva and Pete Dorsey, Shoaf, Pennsylvania.

Displaying their trophy bucks after a Canada hunting trip were John Kikta, ex-mayor and Joseph B. Ferary, 1938. This was perhaps the first vanity license plate in Pennsylvania.

Posing for the photographer on the cannon which sat on Route 21 on the Fayette County side of the Masontown Bridge were Ann, Marge, and Catherine Dockmonovich, Mary Ann Alexander and Antoneta Chankowski.

Shown in front of Pete's Auto Body are Pete Smargie, Jimmy Rye and Pete Micoli.

Young Joe Micoli learning his trade in the early 1950's.

Edward Schaum, owner of the ice plant in Masontown, all dressed up and ready to go.

Unknown granny rocking on the front porch.

Vintage Portraits of the Masontown Area

www.ingramcontent.com/pod-product-compliance
Lightning Source LLC
LaVergne TN
LVHW081354060426
835510LV00013B/1811